THE SEA AT THE DOOR

SYLVIA KANTARIS

The Sea at the Door

For Bill Turner,
with admiration & she-fellow feeling
in this Jigsaw Puzzle (p.69...)
Sylvia Kantaris

SECKER & WARBURG
LONDON

First published in England 1985 by
Martin Secker & Warburg Limited
54 Poland Street, London W1V 3DF

British Library Cataloguing in Publication Data

Kantaris, Sylvia
    The sea at the door.
    I. Title
    821'.914   PR6061.A57/

ISBN 0–436–23070–4

Typeset by Inforum Ltd, Portsmouth
Printed in England by
Redwood Burn Ltd, Trowbridge

For Rachael and Geoffrey

ACKNOWLEDGEMENTS

Anglo-Welsh Review, *Bananas*, *Encounter*, *Equivalencias* (Spain), *Habitat* (Australia), *Helix* (Australia), *London Magazine*, *London Review of Books*, *New Poetry 9* (Arts Council/ Hutchinson), *New Statesman*, *Other Poetry*, *Outposts Poetry Quarterly*, *Poems '83* and *Poems '84* (Lancaster Literature Festival Anthologies), *Poetry Review*, *Proteus*, Rivelin Grapheme anthology of contemporary women poets, *Sesame*, *South West Review*, *Writing Women*.

'Bride Ship' won an award in the National Poetry Competition, 1982, and was broadcast on Radio 3. 'Old Habits' was broadcast on *Poetry Now*, Radio 3.

CONTENTS

THE SEA AT THE DOOR

WATER-COLOURS, CORNWALL

You grow dependent on the weather's moods,
living by courtesy of wind and water
between constraining seas, although sometimes,
in summer, it seems you could slide out easily
across the line where the light blue thickens,
like a colour-wash, before you're beaten back
to shelter by squalls of rain spreading a grey
stain inland. In such weather the peninsula
holds you in small focus. It is a place
for mannikins – their salty, patchwork fields,
their bent shrubs and squat houses huddled away
from the sea's edge, although some stragglers stick
it out too long on sand-cliffs which crumble bit
by bit, under assault, and leave them hanging,
flimsy in the wind like empty matchboxes
until, another day, there's no trace left –
as when a painter thinks maybe he'd rather
not have any hint of humans even half-
way in the picture, and moves the sea up
by an inch or two, to wipe them off.

THE LIGHT AT ST IVES

A myth, he said, set up by the tourist board
to bring in summer visitors, and I admit
I did tend to go on about the light,
but then I think he had a postcard vision of
Hawaiian-yellow sand splodged with red
wind-breakers and bikini blobs, the Island
acid-green against a crude blue sky
and all the colours slipping at the edges.

He probably recalled the jostle and sweat
along the sea-front to the crowded beach,
chips fed to seagulls, St Ives rock,
carved Oriental elephants in Woolworths
and in all the Fore Street tourist shops,
but never walked sheer into the special
clarity of light you find on late September
evenings, approaching from the south.

There is a certain point at which you slip it on
like sea-silk and drift along the Wharf
and up the Digey past the open doors
of houses rooted in deep-sea granite,
between the Bay and the open Atlantic,
washed with cross-currents of marine light
which is mythic and historical and
nothing really to go on about.

Perhaps he never came here in winter
when grey waves beat over Men an Mor
and all the summer restaurants are shut
and the light is the colour of seagulls
flying inland, and the town turns its back.

A NAME

It will die like the sad plash
Of a wave breaking on some distant shore
(Pushkin)

It was the carpet-slippers I noticed first,
over the top of Pushkin in translation.
They were checked, grey and tan, the kind that old men
generally wear, and his ankles were swollen.
There wasn't much else to distinguish him
except that, when he woke, he said he shouldn't
really be on any train, he'd just got on
the Cornish Riviera that afternoon
at Paddington like someone in a dream,
and maybe they would miss him at the hospital.
He pinched himself to prove that he was real
and showed us all his pills, a bottle full
of different kinds like little, coloured pebbles
from a beach, but he had taken none at all
that day, not even for his heart, he said,
and chuckled, fishing out his birth-certificate
as written evidence of what his name was,
then asked us what we thought he should do next.
We phoned from Truro for an ambulance.
On and off since then I've wondered why he chose
Penzance to go to on a one-way ticket
and slept till he was nearly there, and what dream
nudged him back up to the surface just in time
and long enough to tell us what his name was
while he still could, and why there is such comfort
in a name that's written down, under a poem
or just on some old folded document left,
as if by chance, among a heap of clothing
that could be anybody's, at the sea's edge.

SNAPSHOTLAND

In Snapshotland everyone is happy all the time.
It is the promised land where people sit with flasks of tea
on smooth sand by a flat sea and smile and smile and smile.

The sun shines all day long and every day in Kodachrome
or sepia on sandboys and sandgirls who never
stop smiling from the time they first appear, with buckets,
in crisp, gingham pinafores and bonnets on the sea-shore.

Lovers stay in love forever; married couples never
grow tired of each other; everything is always just right.
The dolphins know exactly when to leap into the air
and stay there for the permanent delight of passengers
aboard the pleasure-boat which never passes out of sight.

Nobody in Snapshotland grows old unless they want to,
judging by the way they go on smiling so, in deck-chairs,
on the beach, or in old-fashioned gardens with lavender
and grandchildren here and there – and no-one dies, ever.

Even if they don't appear later, the people are still
always there, smiling through the lavender and dolphins
and the buckets full of pebbles on the same sea-shore.

NIGHT CROSSING

I caught the boat just once
by some strange mismanagement
and stood as it slid out of harbour
silently, unpiloted.
There were no people waving on the shore.
And up and down from end to end
the passengers sat stiff in rows.
None of them had any kind of luggage
or newspapers. They stared at air.
I could have gone on easily with them
but for the drumming in my smuggled suitcase.
Someone tugged the long communication cord.
I still don't know whose noisy heart
reminded me to stop the boat
and moonstep across the strip of marshland
just in time to catch the last train
back here from the border,
or whether there is any point
in sailing out in order to come back
on tracks that disappear under
a smooth, unwinding sheet of blank water.

AFTERBIRTH

I smiled, of course, as mothers do, and waved.
The smile may well have been a bit lopsided
but I was not disturbed, the sea was calm.
I simply didn't reckon with the night storm
crashing round my bed. I saw the sky split
and dreamt the waves collapsed the puny ship.
But you had grown so small, a tiny child
attached to me by one thin, slippery cord.

Such breakers all night long, and you alone
but for this lifeline. Still, I should have known
before your call that you'd arrived intact,
the sea was calm – a gentle swell – you slept.
Your last words, 'We're about to be cut off
Mum', are strange and yet singularly apt.
The cord coils like an eel. I turn and laugh,
remembering that sly clown, the afterbirth.

THE MERMAID IN ZENNOR CHURCH

She is old and half out of her element,
biding time through centuries of Psalms
and Lamentations in a house of worship.

Down below the sea creatures are up to no good,
flickering their immemorial tails
through troubled times and tides of bladder-wrack.

Her siren songs have gone into the wind
to wail around the Rock of Ages
like a woman wailing for the lost men.

Salvaged from the jetsam of the Flood
she stays here, offering herself entirely,
turned aside discreetly from the altar

but shored against the driftwood of the Cross,
her orb a simple mirror in her right hand,
her comb cupped, like a sceptre, in her left.

BRIDE SHIP

The Sailor cannot see the North, but knows
the Needle can   (Emily Dickinson)

I do not envy you your voyage through the silent
and austere solemnity of empty spaces
towards those other, unlocated Capes
which have no shores, or shadows, and are featureless –
like no New England capes or Rock of Ages cleft
to hide your clear eyes from the undivided light.

As wilderness gives way to wilderness I see your slight
form staunch and upright at the helm in bride-white,
your hair parted straight down the middle,
unswerving, trusting nothing but the needle
and the endless Arctic winter of the bone,
singing *Thine for ever!* but utterly alone.

CREIL

Just factories and backs of shabby houses
strung along the railway-track –
the kind of place you wouldn't even notice,
speeding through from Paris to Boulogne
with coffee and long ham-sandwiches,
except for one old woman on crutches
standing in a doorway watching
one more train passing. Creil.
After that, for us, the fog, the hovercraft
and more fog all the way to London,
then the last lap on the Golden Hind
with crowds, beer, BR sandwiches,
even wine – as far as Exeter –
and later just a debris of maxpax,
cellophane and rolling bottles.
I feel sorry for the people who get on at Plymouth.
On the rack, the labels on our little bags
announce that we have been to Paris.
We have our clear and childlike memories
to store against the merging days ahead.
The journey back is largely a blur
except for one old woman, framed, on crutches,
watching our *rapide* sweep out of sight,
who looked as if she might have been at home there
at a grey place with a name like a slate.

THE HOLIDAY

Occasionally, Grandmother, before you died,
you seemed to gather all your strength up
into a single word. You called me 'hard'
when I proposed a holiday with us in town,
because you were too old to be uprooted
and anyway you'd stayed put all your life
except that once when you went off to Blackpool
in your pinafore and had your photo taken,
stiffly, posed against a grey, painted valley
with a stuffed horse. And even then you would
not stay transplanted long enough to see the week out.

Sixty years later when your face was set
in weathered convolutions like a walnut
and I knew every trench and watercourse of it,
I remember how you crooned *The Lord's my Shepherd*
in your nut-cracker voice when you thought
no one was listening, and how it broke
on *death's dark vale*, so that now, when I think
of you in your pinafore in the valley of death,
I see you stuck eternally in Blackpool
with that stuffed horse and imitation scenery,
but gathering your strength to find some way of getting back.

WHAT SHALL WE DO WITH GRANNY?

*Causley asks: 'Did grandmothers come high on the list? We had a lot of
them last year.' They did.*
Observer report on the judging of the Arvon competition, 1982

A glut of grandmothers again this year
before we've even shifted last year's crop.
We've jars on jars of chutney in the cellar
and hundredweights of grannies in the loft.
What's to be done with them? They are too soft
and wizened to be used. In any case
the trace of fustiness puts people off,
and this strain is too sweet for modern tastes
even when they're still quite firm and fresh.
We tried to make a kind of granny wine
but no-one likes the sickly beverage
although they drank it in Edwardian times
before the granny-boom soured our palates.
Those were the days when grandmammas were loved,
along with Golden Pippins and Russets,
when dandelions and cowslips were in vogue
and elderberry wine gushed out of taps,
before we'd heard of *Beaujolais Nouveau*
or lost our taste for sticky home-made cakes.
But grandmothers are out of fashion now.
Grandads haven't yet lost their appeal though . . .

WILLIAM YATES

Elbows stuck out like a Toby-jug,
thumbs in the belt strapped
under his stomach as if to hold it up,
Grandad stood between Margot Fonteyn
and us, and paused
before delivering the verdict:
'Bloody bally!'
At one flick of his wrist
the swan gave up the ghost.
Grandad walked out.
We knew he wasn't really a poet.

'Ah dunna want neoo fancy muck'
was all he said at Christmas
when we brought him gifts
in brown paper bags stuck with Sellotape.
He left them on the sideboard, unopened,
and went out to the yard with his pipe.
Grandmother would not abide smoke.
He knew the rest of us would never dare
to bring him anything but Bruno Flake.

He kept books in a cupboard though –
not just books on lead-mines in the Peak
but atlases, bound copies of Reader's Digest
and Pears' Encyclopaedia
that he'd sent away for once,
paying week by week.
He knew a lot of facts by heart
such as the exact length of the Suez Canal
and how the Pyramids were built,
but he made bricks himself
and didn't mess around with sentiments.

Grandad was a rooted man
although he'd been to London.
Once was enough:
'Yo' munna geoo past Leicester' he warned us,
as if hell started half-way down the map.
At seventy-five he stopped going to work.
At eighty-five he stood behind the gate.
At ninety-odd my grandmother still
made him go out to the yard to smoke.

On the slope of Bradford Dale
In Youlgrave churchyard Yates is laid
Under a conventional phrase
Cut in marble, even though
He would have chosen millstone grit
Without one fancy word on it.

I used to put a bunch of common vetch
there when I visited the spot.
Since Grandmother moved in I slip
a homely weed or two, like charlock,
in amongst the dahlias for his sake.

OLD HABITS

It is the little things that really count,
like cracking finger-joints. I've noticed how
the cracks have spread around the hearth. The walls
are giving up. I do not like the way
the table creaks under the table-cloth.
I wish you would not sigh each time you sit.
Why do you always put spent matches back
into the match-box on the mantelpiece?

You yawn again. The nights are drawing in,
forever closing curtains. It's too soon.
I liked the paint when it was new. Do you
remember covering the chairs with sheets?
I laughed and laughed and said they looked like ghosts.
I wish you would not crack your finger-joints.

THE PHOTOGRAPHER'S EYE

Take this tree for instance, furrowed like an old man's face,
as if an old man had grown into it or else was growing out,
and now a blow-up of his eye, you see
the way it forks out into branches like a tree
and how, in this enlargement of the knotted bit,
there seems to be a man's face with an eye . . .
There comes a point at which you have to stop but it's as if
each single fleck and dot were fathomless –
although of course by focussing on one knot of a tree
you miss the wood. But who could take a forest in?
My friend, I only have one life, one viewfinder, and time
to get one detail of one thicket into focus,
and even then the shutters of the eye cut out
whatever looks too random to touch up and process.

DOUBLE EXPOSURE

Thirty-five years on, we sit outside the kitchen
in summer, reminiscing, and I admire
the wallflowers and the runner-beans distinguishing
your garden from the one next door and from the field
which is still quite deep in grass and buttercups
but has grown out of context since my childhood.

Yet these old-people's bungalows have mellowed now
and look as if they've stood here since before
I thought you capable of really growing old
or could have dreamed that anyone would ever
set up house in this steep field where only grass
and wild flowers grew – and mushrooms in September . . .

And then, in winter, when the snow had fallen
all night long and levelled every bump and hollow,
we children trudged up to the top in wellingtons,
admiring our own footprints,
and sledged down time and time again right through
your kitchen and this very spot where you and I
are sitting now, posed, as in a photograph,
against this season's runner-beans and wallflowers,
smiling at the way things come to pass.

BLUEBELLS

The scent first, faint, almost recognisable,
but not quite – and yet insistent,
as if to make a clearing in the mist
and bring something forgotten into focus.
But even when I came down through the trees
and stood amongst the bluebells
the memory would not come clear of the haze
they spread as far as I could see, like censers –
their stalks strong, taut with sap
and slippery as skin between the fingers.

The stalks were all I really remembered
from the inside of the scene – in May;
the leaves green; filterings of fine rain
mixed with sunlight, and a girl and boy
intertwined like two roots of one tree
in a circle of bluebells.

We couldn't quite distinguish where the sky
ended and the drift of blue began,
the air around us was so stained and misted,
but level with our eyes the stems, in close-up,
were solid and opaline, like flesh,
and almost equally mysterious –
earthed, and yet distilling essences
which slip like coloured light between the fingers.

AFTER THE BIRTHDAY

. . . nor questioned since,
Nor cared for corn-flowers wild,
Nor sung with the singing bird.
Christina Rossetti

After the birthday of your life had come
and gone, and you buried the wild corn-flower
and the singing bird deep in your heart,
how was it that you failed to stop their breath?
Why did the flower grow, and grow more blue
in darkness, harbouring untimely seeds,
and why did the imprisoned bird sing
louder still and fill your mouth with music?
The wild things were always too insistent –
and your heart, fuller and more colourful
in autumn than in spring, though resolute –
but then, in winter, so chastised, so bled
and drained of substance for the pale delight
of God that all your wild life suffocated.
And when the bird had stopped its singing
and the flower had lost its sap, pressed flat
between the pages of your prayer-book,
did you still harbour promises of pulse
for pulse and breath for breath in Paradise
on the cold spring birthday of your death?

PALMISTRY

Other people's lives are as mysterious
as the patterns that are folded in their palms
like complex watercourses – even yours,
although we started out as clear springs
entering one stream and ran together
through one dale until our way divided,
and which of us was which by then or whether
each was half of each is hard to tell.
All the same, the scenes we have encountered
in the years between are as distinct
as our two palms, whatever childish dreams
have run on, underground, unseparated.
Even if we could remember every
shifting aspect of every single course
since then, we'd need a lifetime just to skim
the surface of who we have become, and been,
and histories to trace our long meanderings
through all the branching waterways of friends,
and yet we hold the same first river
very simply in the valley of our hands.

RAIN FOREST, QUEENSLAND

We were like pot-holers down there
with iguanas – ancient moving rocks –
amongst creepers and fluted roots
of trees that shoot up
ages high and fan out finally
to form a more than Gothic vault,
the dark arch pin-holed with light.

The leeches were so suckered to our ankles
we had to hold a match to them
before they dropped off,
leaving a dark stream of blood
which took longer than usual to clot
and ran from our bare heels
like a libation onto darker earth.

Outside, the hot, clammy brightness;
inside, a perpetual sodden shade
rich with decay, the rotten logs
of centuries heaped up criss-crossed
in the aisles and covered over
with fungus and old moss
so you could fall in through the hollow
shell of a tree up to your neck.

There are depths within depths
and scenes hoarded in the camera obscura
of my own quick-change head
from that day twelve whole years back
when my veins pumped different blood.

The forest changes too, over millennia,
but stays
until the trees are cut down
and a natural arch miraculously
sculptured in stone by water
is drowned with its surrounding history
to make a dam.

But I remember the high gloom
of interlacing branches at Numinbah
and at the deepest level where the trees
were parted by the stream
and all its ancient traceries of stone,
the waterfall, lit like stained glass,
before it went under.

I am reminded sometimes in cathedrals here,
my voice dropped to a whisper
even though they may be only
eight hundred years old
say, in the oldest parts,
and the rafters, floor and masonry
are continually under repair.

A forest is recorded dimly
in the branching ribs,
the interlacing arches
and the quatrefoil and sexfoil
in enclosing circles –
as if a shadow-pattern had been cast
and kept intact through generations
and all the little heaped-up lives within them
shed like dead leaves and forgotten.

We only stayed there long enough
to wash the blood down-stream
and catch our breath,
although I've kept impressions in my mind.
But even when the ancient interplay
of light and shade on stone and wood
has been brought inside
momentarily, as if to still it forever,
it is nowhere contained.

TRAVELOGUE

I don't know why it is that lean, lanky
Travelogues of poems with careful detail –
Not too much but just enough to pin
The whole length of the Nile down say –
Generally bore me stiff. It's not as if

I hadn't travelled round the world myself,
By bike, and roughed it in Baluchistan
And rounded capes and horns galore,
Attending to my light meter, and eaten
Whale flesh, raw, and dyed my teeth with betel.

It's not as if I hadn't seen the Taj Mahal
Or stood in awe at Trollfjord or looked
Into a tiger's eye in Kenya and escaped
To tell the tale I never wrote because
It makes me want to yawn. Instead I note

The things that are especially important
Like fading curtains or the way the sun
Illuminates the dust on shelves and chairs
Or picks the silver threads out from the golden
And settles squarely on my pickling jars.

EVIDENCE

As it happened I was sieving gooseberries
to make a purée when the plumber came.
He must have thought it was habitual,

the kind of thing that any normal housewife
would do, or at any rate he winked
as if to say I was believable.

But I still blush to think he could have caught me
in *flagrante delicto* and said so and
the scandal would have been unbearable.

That is, unless he also indulges . . .
What if he winked to show me that he knew
and does it too and our pretence was mutual?

But neither of us *looked* like poets and after all
a poem is not a purée. On top of which a ball-
cock is a ball-cock and quite unequivocal.

THE POLITICS OF GARDENS

Mme Dupin will not tolerate red roses
in her garden because she does not like
their politics, and even pink ones are dubious,
like long-haired students and unclipped hedges.
Some Comrades have a problem with blue flowers
such as lupins, which tend to overreach
themselves the more they're disciplined,
and other people's twitch is always a threat,
the way it tunnels under surfaces
insidiously . . . But lilacs can be worse.
They are alright if planted far enough
away from walls, but radical when too close,
cracking foundations, making the stones sprout.
My next-door neighbour knows what he's about
and stands his flowers to attention for inspection
every morning, straightening their lapels
and whisking dandruff from their shoulders,
always on the watch for alien invaders –
and I must admit that some of my dandelions
have infiltrated his plot and seem intent
on parachuting their unruly seed
over walls, throughout the neighbourhood.
But I am not an active anarchist.
My problem can be summed up in the annual
advance of gooseberries, demanding to be picked
and have something constructive done with them,
whereas I'm more inclined to contemplation.
So this year I shall simply let them rot
back into the earth while I sit out the season
considering the lilac and the stone
and writing poetry until I am grown over
or my own walls, at least, have broken down.

WALLSCAPE

The picture-frame is thin and black.
I hung it on the blank white wall
and tried to think a red geranium
into it, but couldn't make it stick.
At least I made a picture of the wall.

INSCAPE

We remain, clear-sighted
according to our lights
which are unshaded and fixed
above a tubular steel table
in a bare room.
We do not decorate interiors
with pictures to distract us
from the nature of the truth.
A fact is a fact, clear-cut:
it casts no shadow.
We neither cry nor laugh.
Behind our eyes we cultivate
equations in the fluorescent night.
The trees which were a fog
on the horizon of our clarity
have ceased to be a problem since
they were located and reduced to roots.
All hills and valleys have been cancelled out.

THE ENEMY

Everywhere I see it, everywhere –
in the transparency of water
and the brutal nothingness of air.

It is in flames and in the earth and written
on the stones with no names on them now.

We ought to bomb the hell out of it.
Its policies are expansionist.
Nothing has no right to exist.

PAGEANT

Spud wouldn't normally have been enlisted
but numbers were needed for the battle scene
and he would do for that as well as anyone –
as well as Blinker who could reel off all
the dates of all the battles from Thermopylae
to Arnhem, and nearly got on *Brains Trust* once –
or Bobby West who led the soccer team from strength
to strength but looked like all the others in a tunic.
Most of them fell, awkwardly, in combat,
then lay still, theatrically. Only Spud,
resplendent in a papier-mâché helmet,
shoulder to shoulder with Leonidas,
forgot to fall on cue for the *tableau vivant*
and sobbed when he was pushed. They had to silence him,
wide-eyed, mouth open, dribbling like an infant.
Spud wasn't fit to die a Spartan death.

Not that it mattered since the war to end
all wars had ended six whole years back.
All the blackout blinds had been rolled up.
It was a summer evening's entertainment –
the mothers looking on in fifties frocks,
a few shrunken fathers in civvies,
the gangly boys dressed up as warriors,
'frozen' in Hellenic attitudes,
a little like the kids in tin hats since
sprawled around the world on TV newsreels,
some reported missing, some numbered and tagged
before they could have learnt how not to sob
let alone scream, in any language – boys like Spud,
and boys who knew about Thermopylae and such,
and others, distinguished for their footwork,
but all indistinguishably dead.

THE POEMS COMPOSED IN SLEEP

Always perfect, first go – each word
slips into place like a jig-saw piece
without recourse to a Thesaurus.
Last night, for instance, I had this poem
about I don't know what, but it was
magical. There might have been cobwebs
or swans or eiderdowns in it, and yet
it wasn't just romantic moonshine stuff
but relevant – the kind of thing to put
the whole world right before the world knew
what had happened to it. First thing,
as soon as I wake up, I thought,
I'll write it down; the world can wait a bit.
There seems no urgency when you're asleep.

DREAM HOUSE

Not a show-house with wood-look vinyl, a fitted
kitchen and carpets covered with polythene,
but the one I live in nightly, so big
I can flow through the Long Room like water,
noting how the panelling of silver birch
distills the light, and how the radiance lingers
in the air like early-morning haze in summer.
I am happy here, drifting through the countless rooms
I half-forget between times – galleries
and bedchambers and all the secret places
I can rediscover quietly, fingering
brocade and tapestry rippled with such light . . .
I have never needed to look out,
although I think I know the contours of the hills
and each twist of the river by heart, yet don't know
where I am exactly, never having travelled here
by any route I even half-remember.
But in between I guard it like a crystal
I can take out every now and then and almost
look into, regardless of how dark the sky is
or how thick the clots and rinds of outer light.

NIGHT-LIFE

The Prince of Aquitaine could not have known
we spent the night together in my bed.
I was surprised myself, afterwards,
and smiled when I saw the man in Woolworths.

The things I do with mere acquaintances!
And I am a *voyeuse* as well, I watch
the escapades of friends and know about
the undercover rendez-vous they make.

They turn up anywhere – in Africa,
Antarctica and places I had never
even dreamt of where they do things that are
strange or even frankly pornographic.

It's just the gaps that worry me. What if
I also flit around from bed to bed?
You never know what other people know
about the hidden sides of lives you live.

REVENANT

Coming back tonight to this same house, it is a shock
to find somebody else in residence.
The room is not just occupied – it has grown roots:
whole families of creepers are established, trailing
up and down the walls and crawling out from
under chairs, they have been here so long.
'May I just take a look', I ask the occupant,
'to see if any personal effects were left
when someone packed my things and moved them out?'
But I don't recognise the dusty books
or any of the fittings. This new furniture
has seen some years out, standing here, the surfaces
piled up with her accumulated junk.
Her unwashed breakfast-plates are in the sink.
It's pointless looking here for evidence.
'You must have been preoccupied if you forgot
you ever left and never once came back
in all this time to clean the house', she says,
and laughs, as if she thinks I'm making an excuse.
It's clear that one of us is quite confused.
But since I can't remember anything I did
between the dream of living here and this new dream
of coming back, I wash my hands of her strange
shiftlessness, and fade into accommodating mist.

THE FEAST

Twenty-four nights later you were back,
alive, your white hair freshly washed and set.
I heard you rattling pans in the kitchen,
busily preparing for the feast
while we sat out on the verandah
in a place where shadows slice the light
of noon as cleanly as a knife.
The buildings were immaculately white.

But scenes shift rapidly. It was already
evening in another time and place.
The feast was set on snowy tablecloths
outdoors, and you were welcoming the guests,
your family – the living and the dead –
laughing and chatting in your widow-dress.
Such uncles and aunts with waxy cheeks
delicately rouged by the candlelight.

It could have been your wedding feast. I caught
a glimpse of you in white, your hair jet black,
the bridegroom standing in the photograph.
But dreams are not accountable, we were all
young and old and equally alive or dead
no matter where or when, and none of us,
not even I, who seemed to witness this,
appeared to know the haunters from the haunted.

MOTHBALLS

Things had to be preserved – embroideries,
best dresses, lacy curtains, tablecloths
too delicate and beautiful to use
except in dreams perhaps. But in real life
they just stayed, folded, in a shroud of sheets,
protected from the moths by naphthalene.
Each cupboard, chest and wardrobe leaked
a heady scent of mothballs. Things would keep.

Underneath the soil now, in her best at last,
her needlework, at least, is preserved,
and maybe lacy angels trained to trace
the scent of naphthalene down to its source
have wafted her economising soul up
into a gauzy haze of tablecloths,
and heaven is protected for eternity
against battalions of invading moths.

GENIE IN THE BOTTLE

Invisible, Unchanging God,
preserved in vinegar and stuck up
on the highest shelf for all eternity,
I have decided – after much deliberation –
to find the bottle, open it, and set you free
so you can trickle into the sea
or burn as methylated spirit
or frizzle in the sun like black currants.
Your name shall be delivered
to the dandelions and cabbages
and lose its syllable to gain a world.
Then all the saints and all their dark machinery
shall change into a cloud of puff-ball spores
and little scatterings of Mrs Smith
will flower and seed and multiply
and live kaleidoscopically
once you are released, God,
into the common whirl of things
to make your peace with particles of wind.

THE LIFE TO COME

Walls like royal icing, and all the spirits
swathed in veils, like brides, and dreaming, almost,
in a white light reflected from the surfaces –
the marbled lids, the chips of fluorite.

It is a formal, ornamental place
with plaster doves, on vines, encased in glass,
stone flowers as elegant as lilies
and dazzling alabaster effigies.

And yet the spirits are not happy here.
Their sighing is so thin and spectral
that it can't be heard exactly, but I think
they feel neglected in eternity,

forever waiting for the life to come,
like chrysalises in a frosty season
who have forgotten what they were and do not
know what new shape may emerge from their old skin.

SOME UNTIDY SPOT

In memory of Meryon

Tragedies happen anyhow, in corners, when other people
are working or just walking dully along,
as Auden said, thinking of Brueghel's Icarus
who fell into the water in the space between
two glances, and then into the painting, then the poem,
as if the whole Aegean was not wide enough
to hold the impact of the moment of his death.
But this poem is about your son
who was too young to fly like Icarus
and simply walked behind you on an ordinary path
along an ordinary river's edge
then wasn't on the path when you looked back.
So all the lives he might have lived slipped out of him
in ripples and were gone, to all appearances,
yet grow in circles which are not contained
by any accidental river-bank, or even
by the confines of your heart which held him
firmly, safe behind great dykes of love,
but couldn't ring the moment or the one untidy spot.

AS GRASS

And equally, in death we are in life
as in a dream of crossing our own path
and weaving in and out of other lives, as if
there were no end and no beginning to be read
into the humps and mounds of knotted grass.
I can see, easily, that all of us
are grazing on the green flesh of the dead
and breathing our own breath – at least
so long as I have words and am intact
and there is still grass to compare them with.

THE NEW THESAURUS

Not so very long ago a leopard was a leopard,
set firm as a rock or a flea-bitten tabby cat
between leonine verses and leprechauns,
and simply sprinkled, speckled or punctuated with spots
which were established, fixed and constant like the law
of Medes and Persians or an Ethiopian's skin
in their very opposition to things fleeting and uncertain.

Nowadays he stands between Leo and leotard,
splodged and splotched with blotches like his close relation
the Dalmatian, and both of them grow spectral and prismatic
before they turn into a stiff, embroidered mosaic
as durable as the hills or a written constitution,
piebald, stabilised, endlessly immutable,
but also shot with shifting lights and irreversible.

I never bargained for such random variations
in his fixity of spots, and have stopped trusting him
ever since the steadfast Ethiopian lost his skin –
and those old Medes and Persians too (although their names persist
along with Ten Commandments and Twelve Tables in indelible ink)
have long since gone, taking their imperishable law with them,
under hills which stood like fixtures and are endlessly forgotten.

GREETINGS FROM BOMBAY

I have to say first that I have not written you
since last year and am very very sorry
but you know I wished to marry Ludin badly
and her mother has arranged a cousin's boy,
so Ludin told me I can have her sister
and there is one man named Mehmood
the husband of one lovely wife and father
of one beautiful young daughter
he also told me his affair with Ludin
and he wants to marry her (see over).

After several days Mehmood's wife's brother
came to see me with his niece and asked
if I would like to have her mother
because she likes me very much indeed
and I am very happy with the daughter
but Ludin wants to keep on our affair.
I told her I am very very sorry.
How is it with you? I wait impatiently
for news of your affairs with all the family.

SANTA MONA LISA

Even if the enigmatic shadows
at the corners of the lips were caused by
missing molars, and even if she was
a little tired (judging by the stifled
yawn and the dark rings under the eyes)
the flaws compose an image of perfection.
I also have paid homage to the icon
along with other pilgrims from Tokyo,
Christchurch, Rome and Birmingham. I too
have seen the reverential awe in every
eye that eyed her, and have understood why
copies of her image should have gone around
the world like sacred relics. I have seen
the tea-towels near the Parvis Notre-Dame
pegged outside the tourist shops in rows –
hundreds and hundreds of enigmatic smiles
(the line between the breasts slightly misplaced)
and have coolly dried my dishes with
the one, inimitable face.

THE CHOOSING OF THE GROOM

A maid of fourteen brought up in the ways of God
for a celestial destiny, and comely too,
required a plain man, virile still but old enough
to understand the politics of miracles –
or so the Lord implied although, as usual,
He was mysterious about the kind of sign
we could expect. Still, I did as He commanded.
'Go forth and fetch the childless widowers,' I said,
'and let each man prepare to show his rod.'
Word got around in no time and they came
from every shed and workshop, staff in hand,
all hot to try their luck – but Joseph won hands down.
Poetry alone is fit to tell how his staff rose
upright and true, and how the very sap
of Life surged through it, to issue in a dove
of such immaculate snow-whiteness
which on the instant darted Heavenward.
'Thy Will be done, O Lord!' I cried, and thereupon
I, Zacharias, alias Abiathar,
appointed Joseph bridegroom of the maid.
Truly, God performs in impenetrable ways.

TWO PICTURES

One scene is pastoral and you can tell
Eve's wanton disposition from the way
her right hand lingers on the serpent's head,
lovingly, apart from which she's naked.

The other one shows Mary on her throne
holding her firmly swaddled mannikin,
and at her hem the serpent lying dead
and gory, having had its head crushed flat.

If nothing else the little allegory
makes it plain that women's feet had grown
immaculately hob-nailed in the meantime,
under cover of the feminine sublime.

PASTORAL

My farming aunts sent each other calendars
at Christmas, with pictures of thatched cottages
and decorative swallows wreathed around the edges
of uplifting verses on the theme of dark clouds,
silver linings and the golden harvest.

They learnt to bear the burden and the cost
of fodder, mix the pig-swill, scrub the kitchen flags
and count their blessings day by day, with one eye
on a paper Paradise of hollyhocks
and rustics dressed in spotless smocks, the farms
and animals all picturesque, the hay all stooked.

There were no real storms in the calendars
of parables, and no real, cursing menfolk
traipsing through the kitchen with cow-dung on their boots.
No verses mentioned dead beasts, foot-rot, blight
or reckoned up the down-to-earth cost in hard cash.

The aunts were fortified against adversity
by hints of hardships weathered or endured
but held no truck with any Friend in Need
Who could not turn His hand to muck-spreading
and either ruined the harvest, or didn't, depending
on painted rainbows in cloud-cuckoo-land.

GILT-EDGED INVESTMENT

Success comes late except to beauty-queens,
pop-singers and the early-dead like Keats.
It would be good to have it in the bloom of youth
and woo the world with smooth and peachy cheeks
(as well as inner beauty and truth).
It's hard to shrivel indoors through the hay days
just to reap an Indian summer instead
and harder to be wheeled into the limelight
when you're past it and have nothing but
a kernel where there ought to be a head.

FLORAL TRIBUTE

They have arranged themselves like show animals:
the tulips sleek, blood-colour;
the slightly fierce carnations;
the double-daffodils with green tongues.
You'd think they should have squirmed,
shrouded in tissue paper to be delivered
when they are so immaculately groomed,
their stalks taut and strong enough
to stand up to most weathers.

They seem to have stretched since they arrived
and shifted a little bit
although I didn't catch them in the act.
It would be good to keep this splendour
of reds and yellows forever
if they were not already clinically dead.

At least, I suppose they died when they were cut,
though not so you would notice. Maybe there was
just a little shudder in the petals
but decorously managed, *comme il faut*,
as if the point and purpose of the seed time and
the harvest was this ornamental, posthumous début.

TAMED CAT

Civilised by Kit-e-Kat, she merely purrs
and eats most delicately, shaking one back paw
at intervals. Nothing slops over the side.
Her manners are impeccable, even
to the elegant ablutions and the way
she circles round herself before she settles down
to sleep, replete; but when we give her raw meat
she snarls and lugs lumps by the scruff onto the mat
to worry them, making them twitch and jump
like life before she bolts the lot, laps up
the last dribbles of blood and skulks off out
into the jungle, panther-black, her thought
contracted on the taste of still-warm flesh
naïvely bivouacked in shrubs and crevices
across neat lawns, past cultivated borders.

THE NATURE OF THE BEAST

The children in our school are in God's hands.
He has a Plan for each and every one
of them. We look to their salvation on
the Lord's behalf, which does entail some
chastisement of course since human nature
is incorrigibly bestial at base.
The Rock of the Word is our foundation;
Scripture tells us all we need to know,
in black and white, about the work of Satan
and its consequences for the human race.
The room is open-plan, but just peep in,
you won't hear any chattering, they don't
get up to monkey-business when they are alone
in separate cubicles with our unique
accelerated Christian education system
and a little flag which may be raised if
help is needed. Here our children learn respect
for Country and Authority and fear the Lord.
We have a very broad curriculum –
in history, for instance, Victoria
is studied as a pious, upright queen,
a model wife and mother, and a set text.
Those were the good old days of education.
Of course we have advantages such as
computers and speed-learning packages
(this is a multi-million dollar business)
in spite of which we haven't conquered sin.

A little pinched and starved? You are mistaken,
they are drinking at the Fountain of the Lord.
That's just the human frame you're looking at.
The flesh restricts the progress of the soul
until it withers for the soul's salvation.
The spirit is the vessel of the Word.
We do allow a few books, if they're clean,
for instance classics like *Gorilla Hunters*
and biographies of famous fundamentalists
but in the main literature corrupts. An ape
bears no resemblance to a human,
that's a filthy fiction. No, we don't teach sex.

BOSOMS

We are all naked in the sight of God
and the Headmaster, even on the stairs
or in the corridors, but still, it was
not I who nursed an Action Man for comfort,
playing secret agents, his revolver
hard as lead against my back. Take that
you crook, and that, and sign your name in blood.
Smith-Willis saw his sister in the bath
and brought a Cindy Doll to school and sliced
her bosoms off. Now wash your mouth out with soap,
dirty boy. Such filth. In the showers
I watch the mud still trickling down my legs.
Someone screams and no one notices.
Smith-Willis keeps the bosoms in a matchbox
but I don't think they really bring him luck.

THE CHANGE

*The emotionally upset adolescent or middle-aged woman will follow
poetry because it is the only immediately available mode of expressing,
exploiting and dignifying emotional disturbance. The spectacle is
often both absurd and bewildering.*
                              Robin Skelton, *The Practice of Poetry*

I remember how I filled my adolescent verse with emptiness
and brooded over it on windy crags, waiting for Heathcliff,
and wandered, lonely as a poet, from Windermere to Cockermouth
at seventeen, in love, or wanting it,
but anyway emotionally upset.

Today, in middle age already and presumably neurotic,
I turn again to poetry like any silly, lovelorn adolescent
while waiting for the flood and then the ebb-tide of the blood, because
(again presumably) I have no other mode
of getting it and am romantic and absurd.

The old age of womanhood will cure my curse. I shall have found
a way of stiffening my grip on verse when I am high and dry and
changed into an ancient crab with clicking, orange claws
and grasp the fact that in all fundamentals
poetry is one more word for balls.

BIG FLOWERS AND LITTLE

(For Anne Stevenson)

Smoke blooms hugely from the factory chimney
like a giant prize chrysanthemum.
Great stone buds burst open in the quarry
and shed grey petals in the danger zone.
Skyscrapers explode like blown roses
but similes take root in any rubble
and shoot up, lustier than sap, through stalks
of tall and angular machinery
to make a grand bouquet of it.

And then, again, these real flowers, little clichés,
which do bloom, too, at grass-level,
the tiny eyebright, the forget-me-not.

THE RECLUSE

Having chanced upon him by accident
the poet would most certainly have stopped
to ask what hard times had befallen him
and, moved to pity by the sorry state
of house and man, he would have jotted down
the details of his story as he spoke
and would have found the passions of his heart
essentially unspoilt, no doubt. 'Good Sir,'
he would have answered, fighting back the tears
of gratitude, 'the motorway you see
here at my gate was once my father's croft.'
And then he would have told his rustic tale
in simple words with many a weary sigh,
concluding that he bore no grudge because
he had the goat still and wanted for naught.
Or if he spoke in an embittered voice
and swore that he intended to stay put
until he died and take the house and goat
with him, he would have served to illustrate
the sad invasion of the countryside.
What can we say who know the politics
of poetry? That once upon a time
it was original to write about
essential passions of the human heart,
but even then the poet who indulged
was branded as an old, half-witted sheep?

BLUFF

It takes a certain savoir-faire to give a paper on
some area of deconstructionism when
I don't know what it means and can't even read yet.
Naturally I'm also entirely naked.

Still, I stun the auditorium of learned
scholars in the field of studies pioneered
by someone foreign with my startling contribution:
'We need to strip bananas down to basics, Gentlemen.'

And then I swing down from the rostrum without bothering
to register the thunderous ovation, having
no time whatsoever to appear at my next lecture
on post-deconstructionism in Geneva.

I am correctly dressed, in grey, when I arrive
to find the auditorium already packed with
pitifully naked deconstructionists
still stripping bananas in many languages.

THE POET'S WIFE

I help him by taking on the boring jobs
like sorting, filing, typing out and sending to mags.
Try the Big Ones first, he says, but all their editors
are handicapped. (The slips say they're 'unable to publish'.)

The others sometimes shift a paper-clip a bit
before they send them back with a form for a sub.
You have to pay to be a poet, but he packed in his job
after laying six quid out to win five, in a comp.

I don't trouble him with trivialities like FIS
because he has to keep his mind clear and sometimes,
my God, a single line will take up to a week
but if it doesn't seem a moment's thought it's wasted ink.

I like those lines and can't think why he doesn't
write them down and make the best poem ever yet.
Possibly because he uses ballpoint?
It's hard for him when rhymes won't come out right.

Poetry's like ironing, he said – you have to smooth
the creases out. I just get on with it.
Usually he ends up with a crumpled sheet in spite
of getting all steamed up. I'm glad I'm not a poet.

You have to work like mad to make the sentences
sound senseless at the moment, so he writes
'surprising' lines that I can't fathom such as
'Ears like elephantine hand-grenades'.

I don't see the point of it, but he says poets
gaze into a crystal ball like seers and the mists
eventually clear up so that, instead of seeing ordinary leaves,
they see words decomposing in the woods.

And then, at other times, he swears that poetry
should come as naturally as leaves to a tree –
which is another line I like. It's a pity
all his best ones are so contradictory.

But every poet needs to keep in practice
ready for the Big One, and the rubbish
won't be rubbish any more when he's famous.
(Imagine if I just tipped the lot out with his empties!)

You have to think of drink as an investment.
It inspires lines like the one about the elephant
(a major prize-winner, he says, then Faber, then a grant)
but I still think those other lines are far more brilliant.

NOT ALL ROSES

Down on her knees in front of the grate
shovelling the ashes out,
Marriage isn't all roses,
my mother said, her arms
up to the elbows in soot
and burnt-out cinders which she
tipped into a bent grey bucket
while I stood in a cloud
of dust and images
of vistas of imperishable roses
blazing trails of glory
over dump on heaped-up
dump of old wives' ashes.

CAST-OFF

I wouldn't have believed I'd pick out
my old cast-off at a jumble-sale
and actually consider buying it
before I realised and dropped it, quick.

It was as if a bit of who I used to be
had been dug up like old bones from a past
I had forgotten all about although
I felt I ought to have remembered it.

But many an ancient photograph has
my name underneath and someone else's
face in scenes I honestly can't place
which have, by now, become irrelevant.

And yet I wonder if I'd recognise
my old self again by instinct passing
through this space where I am now maybe
and shivering at its strange familiarity.

PROPER VISITORS

My friend's mother always kept a parlour stuffed
with Sunday best furniture for proper visitors
and no one ever sat in it except a dressed-up
china doll which was too perfect to be touched even.
People sat in comfort in the kitchen.

Times have changed but all the same when we came
to this house we carefully disposed the upright chairs
in formal corners of the sitting-room for visitors
who should be seated properly, one here, one there,
but friends sat round the hearth or on the floor.

In time our children also grew considerate
of proper visitors with funny eyes and eyelids
who don't pretend to sip pretending tea and may come
any day and sit, very stiffly, in our own chairs
unless we show correct respect for theirs.

THE OLD POETS

They won't let me go, the old poets,
loud-mouthed still in their graves,
shouting me down.
Even Eliot's drying combinations still
catch the sun's last rays on my line.
But he too had his problems with his forebears –
always at his back and breathing down his neck
until he fixed them
and pinned them down, wriggling,
in his own song.

The woods are alive with dead poets.
There is no tree left that they have not
barked up, ear-marked, fingered
or recycled.
Yeats did for chestnut-trees, root, branch and
bole. They dance to his tune.
And broadbacked figures still
patrol the maytime,
behind the hawthorn,
antique flutes at the ready.

Restless in daylight; pale, unsatisfied
in the dim and the dark hours, they have
had their say and
still come, lusting for more –
old poets, old vampires, hanging on,
their fangs sunk, up to the gum,
in my throat, sucking
the living voice out of me,
hulking their monstrous shadows
through the catacombs of my poems.

A TO Z

All the streets are numbered on the surface.
Because of this I came down to the
Catacombs where there are still a few
Dead old roots of trees to find my way by
Even in the dark. Up there they said
Forget the trees, the plants, the things that
Grew once and would not stay put, and concentrate on
Hexadecimals instead of ancient mud.
I tried but am not angular enough, my
Joints refuse to jerk around the block where
Keepers of the city plot the
Length and breadth of numbers by the clock and
Measure people into rectangles. There
No irregularities are registered, no
Overtones or undertones of lilac mar the
Perfect symmetry of corners, and no
Questions have been asked. Heads click from left to
Right to left and back, depending on
Solutions of equations. I don't fit. There
Tongues have been reduced and cancelled out, but
Underground I sing, and have heard other
Voices, faintly, answering, in strange words
Which I do not understand but know by heart, like
Xhosas calling cattle to the water, and just
Yesterday, it could have been, I thought I heard
Zenske pesme, women's songs of love and birth.

CHINOISERIE

No you are not the lady I adore
Madame, you neither Juliette, nor you
Ophelia, nor Beatrice, nor even
Laure of the gentle eyes, the fair Laure.

My latest love lives far away from here,
In China, at her aged parents' side,
In a tower made of finest porcelain
By the Yellow River where cormorants ride.

Amongst her attributes are eyes that slant,
Feet small enough to cradle in the hand,
Skin brighter than a burnished copper lamp,
Long, tapering, carmine-painted finger nails.

A passing swallow swerves to touch her head,
Framed by the delicate trellis where she stands
Each evening and, just like a poet, sings
Of peach-blossom and other Chinese things.

(Translated from the French of Théophile Gautier)

PIERROT'S MELANCHOLY

For starters, I drink their indifferent eyes.
 If they would only prize
 My bleeding heart, I would kiss
 Their feet to death, in bliss!
Then we chat . . . and Pity overtakes the sighs,
And lastly I offer friendship, with no ties.

Pity steers my offer to be brother, guide;
 But then they think I'm timid,
 Which makes their eyes grow bold:
 'One word, and I'm yours' I'm told
(I believe you). My turn to show the wrinkled hide
Of this world-weary heart, and smile into the void . . .

And suddenly I call off the garrison,
 Alleging some past treason!
 (I've had a narrow escape!)
 Will she write at any rate?
Negative! and I weep for her all autumn . . .
These combinations cause me such exhaustion!

Who will domesticate my heart! Some cure . . .
 I'm so true by nature!
 Meek as a holy sister!
 Come! I'm no smooth talker.
Why so much fuss about a small adventure
Under the sun? In all this rampant verdure . . .

(Translated from the French of Jules Laforgue)

AESTHETIC

Older women or beginners,
I've had a brush with every sort,
Prickly ones and easy pickings.
Now for my interim report:

They are all blooms in varied dress,
Depending on the time of day
They put on proud or lonely airs.
When we cry out and come, *They* stay.

Nothing moves them, nothing angers,
They want us to admire their looks
And drone comparisons with flowers
And keep on using them as such.

Without concern for rings or vows
Let's suck what they can offer us
Regardless of whose distant eyes
Are whose, since they're monotonous.

No time for hope or scenes; pluck on!
Flesh grows old when roses wither;
Let's scale the gamut if we can,
Seeing that there's nothing better.

(Translated from the French of Jules Laforgue)

A BREATH OF SEA AIR

(A corruption of Mallarmé's 'Brise Marine')

Fed up to the teeth and nothing on TV
except repeats. I need to get away
from this dump. Quite honestly I'd rather be
a bird – at least I could get high on sea
and sky out there, exploring the unknown,
instead of feeling bound to mow the lawn
because the sight offends her. I'm up to here
with trivialities; this atmosphere
is no joke for a writer. I've had enough
of babies yelling to be fed. I'm off
across the water, lured by more exotic
music, despite the danger of symbolic
storms and even shipwreck. Nothing can hold back
my sea-soaked heart, intent on a poetic
destiny – estranged, estranged, beyond retrieve,
and the last white flutter of her handkerchief.

FLOWERY LIKE LUST

You say that women
Should suffer polish themselves and travel without loss of breath
Bring precious stones to life embellished with rouge
Sing or be quiet tear the mist
Alas I could not dance in a swamp of blood
Your face shines from the other side from the happy bank
Everything living rots

You say that women
Should be able to cast off everything even
The suckling still resistant
To love
Your face turns blue as your fortune grows
And personally I want to die sprawled in sage
Arrogantly bad in exiled immobility

You say that women
Should destroy themselves to avoid giving birth
And wait wait for the solid snaking delight
Alas I do not like making love on the carpet
Beelzebub coos in pigeons' throats
Your ring burns my thigh
The emerald is the virginity
Of the rich

You say that women
Are made to nurture
The repentant smoke puffing in church
The pale and pregnant sows studded with soiled bristles
Heads cut off as well and why not after all
Astonishing polar nights of sanguinary silences
I think I can let you go now

Your legs fly high in the cracking
Sacristy
Of knees
Like so many preachers
I am very glad to have a hat on my head
Even if your urine does contain all the enchantment of marriage
You say that women are canons of ecstasy
I alas relish nothing but death

(Translated from the French of Joyce Mansour)

DO YOU REMEMBER . . .

Do you remember the sweet scent of plantains
How strange familiar things can be after a departure
The dreariness of food
A dismal bed
And the cats
Do you recall the cats with shrill claws
Shrieking on the roof as your tongue explored me
And arching their backs as your nails scored me
They vibrated when I yielded
I have forgotten how to love
The doleful bubbles of delirium have vanished from my lips
I have abandoned my mask of leaves
A rose-bush is dying under the bed
I no longer sway my hips among the rubble
The cats have deserted the roof

(Translated from the French of Joyce Mansour)

JIGSAW PUZZLE

Quite easy with a picture to go by,
matching light with sky and shade with tree –
and people with human anatomy –
but far more difficult if all you have
are pieces, and the overall design is lost
so that you have to play at being God.
The frame is not much trouble, there is a neat
finality about straight edges
bordering a scene as if to keep
whatever may evolve, with time, intact.
But then the bits of eye and hand and wood
tend to get mixed up until they're found
to fit well in a certain place, as if
they were predestined to interlock,
although sometimes a loop of hair turns up
by accident or error in a clump of grass
or branches probe into a piece of head.
At that point the scene becomes a senseless
composition of missing links and gaps
and shapes which won't fit anywhere unless
by sheer coincidence of circumstance.
It's all a case of fumbling in the dark
towards a meaningful relationship
between assorted meaningless components,
and even if I get there, by luck,
the more I look at it the more I am
inclined to break the whole creation up
and make a simple cube with building-blocks.

WINTER TIME

I don't put the clock back. I just stop it
for an hour and let time do the catching up
while I prepare myself for a new début.
A winter wind is timed officially
to strip the cherry boughs on cue.
Tomorrow I may hunch my back
and sweep the dead leaves into little heaps,
cantankerously, muttering to myself.
Tomorrow I may gather cats for comfort.
But this is the witching hour between times,
when warts grow magically like mould on bark –
an hour to gut the turnip of its pulp
and carve an admirable hollow head
fit for Hallowe'en, the mouth a gap,
the eyes triangular, their sight
a trick of guttering candlelight.
It is a winter mask to set beside the hearth
and contemplate. Before the snow drifts
lightly over chimney-pots, like ash
over a foliage of photographs,
I ponder on the luck of wearing it,
in time, deaf to the ticking clock,
indifferent to all that comes to pass,
as to a wall on which a fitful lantern casts
shadow-patterns, powdering like moths.